YODER DEPARTMENT STORE
State Road 5, Box 245
Shipshewana, IN 46565
(219) 768-4887
www.yoderdepartmentstore.com

The Garden Table

ELEGANT OUTDOOR ENTERTAINING

Kees Hageman

Elisabeth de Lestrieux

Jan Lagrouw

FRIEDMAN/FAIRFAX

PUBLISHERS

A FRIEDMAN/FAIRFAX BOOK

Friedman/Fairfax Publiehers

15 West 26 Street

New York, NY 10010

Telephone (212) 685-6610

Fax (212) 685-1307

Please visit our website: www.metrobooks.com

This 2000 edition published by Michael Friedman Publishing Group, Inc.

©1992 Terra Publishing Co. Ltd., Netherlands/Lannoo, Belgium

Library of Congress Cataloging-in-Publication Data available upon request.

ISBN 1-58663-011-3

Editors: Rachel Simon and Susan Lauzau
Art Director: Jeff Batzli
Art Designer: Jan Melchior
Photography Editor: Wendy Missan
Production Manager: Karen Matsu-Greenberg

Color separations by Radstock Reproductions
Printed in Hong Kong by Midas Printing Co. Ltd.

1 3 5 7 9 10 8 6 4 2

Distributed by Sterling Publishing Co., Inc.
387 Park Avenue South
New York, NY 10016-8810
Orders and customer service (800) 367-9692
Fax: (800) 542-7567
E-mail: custservice@sterlingpub.com
Website: www.sterlingpublishing.com

CONTENTS

Introduction

Food and fresh air are inseparable companions, and this union is joyfully celebrated in *The Garden Table*, a pictorial account of the garden as dining room. Set in a relaxed and rambling country garden, the story begins with the chill remnants of winter and continues through all the exuberance of the ripening seasons to close with the fading glow of autumn.

The lush setting and the seasons inspired the food, which celebrates the special generosity of the evolving year. Even in winter, the mood of eager anticipation triggers tempting menus of unrivaled elegance, which are intended to be enjoyed inside and accompanied by hothouse flowers. As winter turns into spring and pale green bulb tips emerge, early vegetables give a welcome foretaste of the approaching growing season. Then follows the abundance of summer, to be enjoyed at elegant outdoor dinner parties or casual picnics.

This chronicle of a country garden throughout the year has been beautifully recorded in breathtaking landscapes and luscious flower portraits and still lifes, all with more than a hint of the Dutch Masters' techniques. Foliage, blooms, and dishes from simple to extravagant combine in an exquisite tapestry of seasonal bounty.

A visual feast and a treasury of exquisite recipes, *The Garden Table* is sure to encourage you to forsake the dining room and move the table outdoors, where leaves and flowers take the place of walls and the ripening fruits, vegetables, and herbs dictate the daily fare.

White in Winter

Even when winter brings no snow, a profusion of white and green ornamentation creates a feeling of crisp air and cool days. Ivy's glossy, evergreen leaves combine beautifully with the hothouse blossoms of cranberrybush, sweet-smelling lilac, and ornamental onion flowers from the garden. A pyramid of green apples echoes the vibrant colors and scents the air. For an elegant winter celebration, serve Chilled Oysters with shots of vodka, syrupy with cold, in frosted glasses.

CHILLED OYSTERS

24 oysters on the half shell
2 tablespoons finely chopped or
   snipped chives
½ cup (125ml) crème fraîche
   freshly ground pepper, preferably
   white
   freshly squeezed lemon juice
1 teaspoon powdered gelatin
1 small jar black caviar or lumpfish roe

Rinse the oysters in a sieve over a bowl and reserve the liquid. Reserve the shells and clean them thoroughly. Drain the oysters on paper towels.

Combine the chives in a small bowl with the crème fraîche and season with pepper and drops of lemon juice to taste.

In a measuring cup, combine the reserved oyster juice with enough water to make ½ cup (125ml), and heat in a small pan. Sprinkle with the gelatin and stir over low heat until the gelatin is dissolved and the liquid is clear. Pour into a small bowl and refrigerate until nearly set.

Place a teaspoonful of the crème fraîche mixture into every oyster shell, top with one oyster each and cover with a little oyster jelly. Chill in the refrigerator to set the jelly properly. Serve with a small dollop of caviar.

Makes 24

Trapping the Sun

Bulbs have been gathering strength to push their beautiful flowers through the cold earth. And now wintry sunlight rewards us by playing on brilliant drifts of snowdrops and crocuses. Even as you get this first glimpse of the coming spring, you may still need to warm yourself with a bowl of this golden broth.

FISH BROTH WITH OYSTERS

18 oysters on the half shell
5 cups (1.25 litres) Court Bouillon
   (recipe at right)
4 tablespoons (60g) unsalted butter,
   cut into small cubes
   salt and freshly ground pepper

Remove the oysters from the shells and drain on paper towels.

Heat the bouillon until nearly boiling, then whisk in the butter to very slightly thicken the bouillon. Season to taste with salt and pepper.

Place 3 oysters in each of 6 soup bowls and pour the hot bouillon over the oysters.

Serves 6

Court Bouillon

Court Bouillon is a flavorful poaching liquid.

6   cups (1.5 litres) water
1   cup (250ml) white wine
1   leek, well rinsed and roughly cut into
      pieces
2   onions, thickly sliced
4   cloves garlic, bruised
4   bay leaves
1   large carrot, peeled and thickly sliced
      small handful parsley and celery
      leaves
2   cloves
      dash of vinegar or the juice of half
      a lemon
      thyme, rosemary, or tarragon sprigs
      (optional)

Combine all the ingredients in a large pan
and bring to a boil. Simmer for 30 minutes
and strain.

When using for fish, shrimp, crayfish, lobster, or crab, make sure the liquid never actu-
ally boils, but stays just at a near-boil.

For a nice flavor variation, add 2 coarsely
chopped green peppers, celery stalks, celeriac, and/or coriander seeds. Court Bouillon
may also be used in vegetarian soups. When
cooking vegetables, add a generous dash of
extra virgin olive oil to the bouillon to give
the vegetables an attractive glossiness.

Food for the Soul

Below ground, winter is a time of renewal. And in the kitchen we like to celebrate earthy pleasures: there are truffles tossed with golden-fried potatoes and tagliatelle, as well as stacks of crispy-edged buckwheat blinis, crowned with caviar and crème fraîche. Such indulgences strengthen and sustain the soul during the coldest season.

TAGLIATELLE WITH POTATO AND TRUFFLE

3 tablespoons extra virgin olive oil

2 large potatoes, cut in half and thinly
  sliced

  salt and freshly ground black pepper

1 pound (500g) tagliatelle

1 truffle or ½ pound (250g) mushrooms,
  thinly sliced and cooked in a little oil

Heat 2 tablespoons of the olive oil in a heavy-based frying pan, add the potatoes, and cook over moderate heat until the potatoes are cooked through and golden brown. Season with salt and pepper and keep warm.

Meanwhile, cook the pasta in a large pot of boiling salted water until just tender, then drain. Place the pasta in a frying pan together with the remaining tablespoon of olive oil and season with salt and pepper, tossing well. Serve on heated plates, with potatoes, shavings of truffle, or with the cooked mushrooms.

Serves 6 as a first course

BLINIS WITH CAVIAR

Cook blinis in a special little blini pan, about 4 inches (10cm) in diameter, or in the metal rings used to fry eggs.

1 cup (250ml) milk, warmed

¾ cup (90g) buckwheat flour

1 cup (125g) plain flour

½ ounce (15g) powdered dry yeast
  pinch of salt

1 egg white

2 tablespoons (30g) unsalted butter,
  melted

  crème fraîche or sour cream, to serve

  caviar or lumpfish roe, to serve

To prepare the blinis, combine the milk, both sifted flours, yeast, and salt in a bowl and stir until it becomes a smooth batter. Add more milk if necessary.

Cover loosely with a clean cloth and let stand in a warm spot for 3 hours. (You may use an oven with only the pilot light on.)

Beat the egg white until stiff but not dry and fold into the batter. Brush a little of the melted butter into a blini pan or frying pan and cook 2 tablespoons of the batter at a time over moderate heat until brown on one side. Flip over and cook the other side. Keep warm in a low-heat oven until all the blinis are cooked. Use more melted butter as necessary to cook the remaining blinis.

Serve with crème fraîche or sour cream and caviar as desired.

Makes about 12 to 15 blinis
Serves 4 to 6 as an appetizer

Awakenings

With the promise of spring there is an awakening of new life. A trip to the flower market inspires us to bring back armfuls of flowers in riotous colors. This is no time for tasteful monochromatic displays—tulips are triumphant across the spectrum, daffodils twirl in golden skirts, ranunculus and bluebells add splashes of contrast, while jonquils add fragrance to the vivid display.

On the table, too, we find a new freshness and lightness. The coral tones of seafood make a delicious contrast to the vivid green vegetables in this delicious salad. Here, a tender first harvest of broad beans are tossed with broccoli florets and crunchy snow peas, along with assorted seafood.

Caught between seasons, there is a kind of wistful glory in a pitcher that combines the indoor dazzle of clivia, the still-green blossoms of cranberry-bush, the gentle mauve of sweet lilac, and a burst of grape hyacinth and forget-me-nots, which remind us of the retreating winter.

SALAD OF VEGETABLES AND SEAFOOD

- 2 pounds (1kg) mixed green vegetables, such as peas, broad beans, snow peas, green beans, and broccoli florets
- 3 tablespoons walnut oil or extra virgin olive oil
- 1 tablespoon raspberry vinegar or fresh lemon juice
  salt and freshly ground black pepper
- 1½ pounds (750g) mixed seafood, such as scallops, shrimp, and mussels

Cook the vegetables separately as desired, but make sure they're not overcooked. To preserve the bright green color when cooking the vegetables, plunge them into boiling salted water, then cook them as briefly as possible. To "set" the green color, refresh under cold running water. When all vegetables have been cooked and cooled, combine them in a bowl.

Make a dressing by whisking the oil, vinegar, salt, and pepper together. Pour over the vegetables, toss well, and allow to stand for 1 hour.

When ready to serve, bake, fry, or steam the seafood separately. Arrange the cool vegetables on a platter and spoon the warm seafood on top. Serve immediately.

Serves 6

A Full Circle

As spring arrives we use every bowl, vase, and platter to display all that the new season has to offer, even while continuing to celebrate the lush fruits of autumn and winter. Luminous red apples and pomegranates pick up on the lovely color of gracefully arching tulips. One dried gunnera leaf brings us full circle, its presence a reminder of the cycle of life.

A Few Tips…

This still life is a simple yet stunning way to show off the new season's produce. Tiny ears of wild asparagus are draped in front of fat, white asparagus spears and spring onions. Create a light and aromatic repast with new potatoes sliced up with truffles and tender chicken.

FRIED POTATOES WITH TRUFFLE AND CHICKEN

Although fresh truffles are best, they can also be frozen successfully. The texture will be softer, but the flavor is the same. To freeze, simply clean in cold water, dry well, and wrap securely in foil before placing in the freezer. For the following recipe, there should ideally be the same number of slices of truffle, potato, and chicken. The amount of potatoes and chicken you'll need depends entirely on the amount of truffle you have at your disposal.

truffle

potatoes, peeled

chicken breasts, boned

unsalted butter

extra virgin olive oil

salt and freshly ground black pepper

dressing of your choice (see below)

Thinly slice the truffle and count the number of slices. Set aside. Cut as many thin potato slices as there are truffle slices and set aside between layers of paper towels.

Cook chicken breasts in unsalted butter in a frying pan until just done. Set aside to cool. Cook the potato slices in extra virgin olive oil until golden and cooked through. Season with salt and pepper and drain on paper towels.

Cut the cooled chicken breasts into thin slices, the same number as truffle and potato slices. Season with salt and pepper. Arrange the truffle, potato, and chicken slices in an overlapping circle on a platter. Drizzle with dressing and serve immediately.

Dressings

- When it comes to dressings, anything goes. If you like a sweeter dressing, use a little sugar. If you're partial to mustard, why not add some? You'll want to make sure to keep a good balance, however. Too much vinegar or lemon juice, for example, can overwhelm a delicate dish. And the flavor of the wine you're drinking can also be affected by a strong sweet or sour flavor.

- Oil is the most important part of a good dressing—buy the very best that you can afford. Since olive oils can be quite expensive, it's worthwhile shopping around. There are many other oils that work well, including sunflower oil and grapeseed oil. Use nut oils such as walnut or hazelnut oil for a special flavor. For an Asian taste, use sesame oil. Sesame oil has a very strong flavor, so it is best used in combination with an oil that is more bland.

- One simple dressing is to combine 3 or 4 parts oil with 1 part vinegar. Remember that salt does not dissolve in oil, so start making a dressing by whisking a small quantity of salt with the vinegar or lemon juice. When the salt is dissolved, whisk in the oil. Add pepper and finely chopped herbs such as chives, parsley, or thyme, as desired.

- Balsamic vinegar makes for an interesting, though expensive, change. Just a few teaspoons gives a deep and satisfying flavor.

- Don't dress a green salad until ready to serve, so that you preserve crispness. When dressing a more robust salad, such as potato, it's a good idea to add the dressing while the vegetables are still hot.

Salad
with
Herbs
and
Flowers

Choose one color to set the tone for your table and let a salad of mixed leaves and edible flowers provide the lively counterpoint. Here, freshly picked nasturtiums, violets, honeysuckle, red-veined sorrel, and pansies add pleasing flavor and color.

The various blues of the spring sky are found in these flowers, from the midday clarity of grape hyacinths to the velvety evening blue of irises.

A GARDEN SALAD

Exotic salad greens make a sophisticated addition to these colorful flowers and piquant herbs. Red-leaf lettuce, baby spinach leaves, romaine, arugula, curly endive, and radicchio are all popular and easy-to-find options. Or try mesclun, a mix of salad greens that may include lettuces, choi, kales, mustard greens, and endives. The exact mix depends on the palate it was designed to please.

A Feast for the Senses

Plant lacy white flowers, such as this Queen Anne's lace, and celebrate spring with a lunch amidst their elegant blooms. Loose knots transform a simple white tablecloth into a romantic element in a garden idyll. Fresh golden rolls or brioches complement a delicate terrine made with the last of winter celeriac and fresh spring asparagus.

POTATO, ASPARAGUS, AND CELERIAC TERRINE

What a pretty and elegant dish for a party!

1 pound (500g) potatoes, peeled and cubed

3 tablespoons (45g) unsalted butter, at room temperature

3 egg yolks
salt and freshly ground pepper, preferably white

2½ tablespoons powdered gelatin

½ medium celeriac, peeled and cubed

1 cup (250ml) heavy cream

15 green or white asparagus spears, trimmed

½ pound (250g) thinly sliced prosciutto

4 extra potatoes, cooked whole and sliced

Cook the potatoes in lightly salted boiling water until tender and then drain. Mash until smooth with the butter and egg yolks and season with salt and pepper. Don't use a food processor, this will make the mixture pasty. Dissolve half the gelatin in a little hot water and mix into the potato purée.

Cook the celeriac in the heavy cream until tender; drain and reserve the cream. Purée, using as little cream as possible, and mix in the remaining gelatin, dissolved in a little hot water. Season with salt and pepper.

Plunge the asparagus into lightly salted boiling water and cook until tender, but still crisp. Drain and cool on paper towels.

Grease a 12-inch (30cm) cake pan with olive oil and line with the prosciutto so the slices overlap. Leave the excess hanging over the edge of the pan. Spoon a layer of potato purée into the pan, press a layer of asparagus into the purée, then a layer of celeriac purée, followed by slices of potato. Continue in this fashion until all the ingredients have been used. Fold the overhanging edges of the prosciutto over to enclose the filling securely. Put the pan in the refrigerator, and let it set for several hours. Serve at room temperature and slice with a thin, sharp knife.

Makes 15–20 slices

Dreaming of Tarts

When rhubarb stalks turn crimson and hyacinths perfume the air, it's time to make these pale pink tartlets of rhubarb jelly. Sweetened with honey and lightened with cream, they make a pretty gift, gathered in pale tissue paper and fastened with a flower.

RHUBARB TARTLETS

- 1 package of frozen puff pastry
- 2 pounds (1kg) rhubarb
- 1 cup (250g) sugar (or more)
- 1 tablespoon honey
- 4 tablespoons powdered gelatin
- 1 cup (250ml) heavy cream
  sugar, to taste

Preheat oven to 375°F (190°C).

Roll out the pastry and use it to line 12 lightly greased tartlet tins. Line with foil and weigh down with baking weights or dried beans. Bake for 10 minutes, then remove the foil and weights and bake another 10 minutes or until fully cooked and golden.

Rinse the rhubarb and cut into ¾-inch (2cm) pieces. Place in a nonreactive pan with the sugar and add just enough water to cover the rhubarb. Bring to a boil. Once boiling, taste and see if you need any more sugar. Add the honey.

When the rhubarb is nearly tender, remove a quarter of the liquid to a bowl and add 1 tablespoon of the gelatin. Stir until the gelatin is dissolved, then set aside to cool. Add the remaining 3 tablespoons gelatin to the rhubarb in the pan, stir until dissolved, and set aside to cool.

Beat the heavy cream with sugar to taste until stiff, and fold into the cooled rhubarb when it is starting to set. Spoon this mixture into the prepared tartlet shells. Spoon the clear rhubarb jelly over the top and allow to set completely in the refrigerator.

Makes 12 tartlets

You can make this even more delicious by filling the tartlets with crème patissière first.

Crème Patissière

- 2 cups (500ml) milk
- 1¼ cup (300g) sugar
- 1 vanilla bean
- 5 egg yolks
- ⅔ cup (75g) sifted flour

Combine the milk, ⅔ cup (150g) sugar, and the vanilla bean in a pan and bring slowly to a boil. Meanwhile, beat the egg yolks with the remaining sugar until pale and creamy, then fold in the flour.

Remove the vanilla bean from the hot milk and pour the milk into the egg yolk mixture, stirring constantly. Transfer the mixture to the pan and cook over low heat, stirring constantly, until thickened.

Allow to cool and spoon into the tartlets. Next, spoon in the rhubarb and cream mixture and top with clear rhubarb jelly.

The Subtleties of White

White in the garden offers its own kaleidoscope of pattern and texture; it highlights the habit of plants, their leaf form, and their floral display. Here, sweet pea grows into a green flower-flocked wall behind an airy border of baby's breath in full flower, while loosestrife lends a slender ear and silver leaf.

Tumbling onto a garden path, white, cream, and yellow combine beautifully. The fuzzy silver leaves of lamb's ears steal the show with their tactile allure.

Gold Leaf and Gilt Edging

Pale gold adds warmth to a white and green scheme. Honeysuckle glorifies a gateway and welcomes guests with its sweet perfume, while lady's mantle spills glowing flowers at their feet. Behind the hedge, Salvia glutinosa *adds its drooping spikes to a scene that creates its own pervasive golden light.*

Elsewhere, 'Golden Dwarf' goldenrod shows off its fine gold foliage, and highlights the huge halos of silvery lilac ornamental onion.

Asparagus...

The first prized asparagus of spring has given way to a summer abundance. Grilling or frying intensifies the unique flavor of asparagus' delicate spears, a taste that is complemented by the richness of olive oil, bacon, eggs, or cheese. Wild asparagus is rarer, justifying a little extra effort to prepare a dish of stuffed mushroom caps—which retain an earthy appeal.

MARINATED MUSHROOM CAPS FILLED WITH WILD ASPARAGUS

Marinade

⅓ cup (80ml) walnut oil

2 tablespoons red wine vinegar

1 teaspoon sugar
   pinch of salt

1 clove garlic, finely chopped

Mushroom Caps

8 large mushrooms with stems

¼ pound (125g) bacon or smoked speck,
   cut into small cubes

4 ounces (125g) white cocktail onions,
   drained and rinsed

½ pound (250g) wild asparagus
   salt and freshly ground black pepper

Make the marinade first by combining all the ingredients in a bowl and whisking well. Set aside.

Remove and reserve the mushroom stems and clean the caps with a damp cloth. Place the caps in the bowl with the marinade and toss gently. Leave to marinate for several hours. Chop the reserved mushroom stems.

Preheat oven to 350°F (180°C).

Place the bacon in a frying pan and cook over moderately low heat, stirring frequently, until the fat is running and the bacon is crisp and golden. Remove with a slotted spoon and drain on paper towels.

Remove all but 1 tablespoon of the bacon fat and add the onions to the pan. Sauté until golden, then add the chopped mushroom stems and cook for 2 minutes. Add the asparagus and sauté until hot. Return the bacon cubes to the pan, season with salt and pepper, and add a few tablespoons of the marinade.

Meanwhile, place the mushroom caps in a dish in the oven and bake for 5 minutes, or until warm. Place the caps on a platter and fill with the asparagus mixture. Serve immediately.

Serves 4 as a first course

FRIED GREEN ASPARAGUS WITH CHEESE

Green asparagus needs very little trimming: simply remove the woody ends. Only peel the stems if the asparagus seems old.

You can leave the asparagus whole, or cut it into large or small pieces. Fry in butter, in a combination of unsalted butter and olive oil, or just oil, but not for too long, since they need to stay crisp. If you like, add a finely chopped small onion or shallot. Use plenty of freshly ground black pepper. When really hot and golden brown, sprinkle with grated cheese.

Toss well and serve immediately. Or place the cooked asparagus in a dish and top with some of your favorite cheese. Bake in a 400°F (200°C) oven until the cheese melts.

A Pod of Poppies

Poppies, with their crêpe paper petals and pepper-pot seed capsules, have both beauty and curiosity value to enchant the gardener. This lilac poppy is blotched in the center with deep purple. Don't pick all the pods for indoor flower arrangements; leave dozens to self-seed and expand your field of dreams.

Summer Harvest

A study in green and pink, this summer bowl of flowers combines graceful peonies with the pale heads of lady's mantle, nodding green-white umbels of wild hydrangea, and a botanist's delight of leaves—variegated, needled, and serrated.

One of the great rewards of the garden is to gather a rich harvest of flowers, fruits, and vegetables. Glossy-skinned eggplants, zucchini, and sun-ripened melons delight the eye as much as the palate and lend their forms to striking arrangements on platters and in bowls.

Have Your Cake...

Long summer afternoons in flower-filled gardens are made for indulgence. Pile buttery tarts high with jewel-like berries and display them alongside the richest, most sinful chocolate tortes.

Terra-cotta pots filled with plants grown as standards or vines twined up a bamboo pole create charming centerpieces in any garden setting. Best of all, they can be moved to accent your surroundings no matter where you decide to set the table.

Fruit Feast

Summer fruit makes an irresistible addition to the garden table. Pile it in glass urns, bowls, and stemmed plates to best display its natural beauty. Stacks of golden crêpes invite each guest to choose his or her own luscious fresh fruit filling.

CRÊPES WITH SUMMER FRUIT

1 cup (125g) flour
  pinch of salt
3 large eggs, lightly beaten
3 tablespoons (45g) melted, unsalted butter
1½ cups (375ml) milk
4 tablespoons (60g) unsalted butter to cook the crêpes

Sift the flour and salt into a large mixing bowl. Combine the eggs, melted butter, and milk in a separate bowl. Make a well in the center of the flour and slowly pour in the egg mixture. Stir with a wooden spoon, gradually blending in the flour until well combined and there are no lumps. Allow batter to rest in a cool place for at least 2 hours.

Melt a little of the remaining butter in a small crêpe pan over medium heat. When the butter begins to sizzle, pour a thin layer of batter into the pan and cook for about 1 minute, or until bubbles start to appear on the surface, before turning. Cook the other side for 30 seconds. Repeat with the remaining batter, stacking the crêpes and layering them with wax paper, on a plate in a 240°F (120°C) oven.

Makes about 18–24 crêpes

Fill crêpes with a selection of fruits and serve with ice cream or a large dollop of crème fraîche or sour cream. Crêpes are also very nice with fruit coulis: purée fruit of your choice (such as raspberries) and add confectioner's sugar to taste and a little squeeze of fresh lemon juice to bring out the flavor.

A Rosy Cheek

Some of the season's best fruits are provided by the rose family—strawberries, raspberries, and blackberries are all Rosaceae, and are delicious in combination. Spike a berry salad with the tingle of mint. Or use your summer berries in this delicious tart.

STRAWBERRY AND BLACKBERRY TART

Sweet Short-Crust Pastry

- ¼ cup (75g) sugar, or more
- 10 tablespoons (150g) cold unsalted butter, cut into pieces
- 1¾ cups (220g) flour, sifted
  pinch of salt

Filling

- 1 pound (500g) strawberries, halved
- 6½ ounces (200g) blackberries
- ½ teaspoon powdered gelatin
- ¼ cup (60ml) apple juice or white grape juice

Combine the sugar, butter, flour, and salt in a bowl and rub between your fingertips until the mixture resembles coarse crumbs.

Quickly knead into a smooth ball. You can also combine the sugar, butter, flour, and salt in a food processor and pulse until the mixture resembles coarse crumbs. Process until the mixture comes together, remove, and knead briefly on a lightly floured surface until you have a smooth dough.

Flatten slightly and place in the refrigerator, wrapped in plastic wrap or foil, for 30 minutes.

Preheat oven to 400°F (200°C).

Roll dough out on a lightly floured surface to a 10-inch (25cm) circle and fit into an 8–9-inch (20–23cm) greased tart tin with removable bottom. Prick the bottom all over with a fork and bake until fully cooked and golden brown. Remove from the oven and cool.

Fill the tart shell with the fruit. Dissolve the gelatin in a little hot water and mix with the fruit juice. When starting to set, brush over the tart.

Serves 6 to 8

Contrasts and Harmonies

Tangerine-toned poppies and deep mauve bluebells—each vibrant color brings out the strength of the other. Red currants, pears, and a lapis-blue platter are combined to create a similar effect. Despite the vivid presentation, this tart is a delicate experience—gently poached pears sit in frangipane cream, barely contained by a crumbling sweet crust. Afternoon tea beckons.

Pear Tart with Frangipane

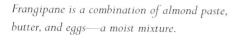

Frangipane is a combination of almond paste, butter, and eggs—a moist mixture.

Frangipane

- 13 ounces (400g) almond paste
- 8 tablespoons (125g) unsalted butter
- 3 large eggs

Tart

- 1 quantity sweet short-crust pastry (see recipe page 50)
- 4 cups (1 litre) water
- ½ ounce (150g) sugar, or more
- 4 pears, peeled, cored, and thinly sliced red currants to decorate

Make the frangipane first by combining all the ingredients in a food processor and processing into a compact, stiff mixture.

Preheat oven to 400°F (200°C).

Roll the pastry out on a lightly floured surface to a 10-inch (25cm) circle and fit into a 8–9-inch (20–23cm) greased tart tin with removable bottom. Prick the bottom all over with a fork and bake for 20 minutes. Remove from the oven, allow to cool a little, and fill with the frangipane. Turn the oven down to 350°F (180°C) and bake for 20 minutes or until the pastry is golden and fully cooked. Allow the tart to cool.

Bring the water and sugar to a boil. Add the pear slices and cook gently for 2 minutes.

Drain and cool, then arrange the slices, slightly overlapping, onto the frangipane-filled tart. Garnish with red currants.

Serves 6 to 8

Poppy Parade

The perennial Oriental poppy flounces through early summer in a variety of paper-thin, rumpled dresses. Names such as 'Orange Glow' and 'Indian Chief' tell of bright colors, and 'Goliath' (also known as 'Beauty of Livermore') is resplendent in wide scarlet skirts. Those who love pastels may prefer 'Cedric's Pink', 'Juliane', and 'Karine', while the undecided can plant bicolors such as 'Flamingo'.

Orange-pink shrimp echo the color of certain poppies—here, vol-au-vents, baked pastry shells, are filled with meltingly tender shrimp ragout.

VOL-AU-VENTS WITH SHRIMP RAGOUT

  8 ready-made vol-au-vents
  1 quantity roux (recipe opposite)
24 cooked shrimp, peeled and deveined

Preheat oven to 350°F (180°C).
  Make the roux, add the shrimp, and allow to heat through while the vol-au-vents warm in the oven for 5 minutes. Divide the mixture between the pastries and serve immediately.

Serves 4 to 8

Roux

4 tablespoons (60g) unsalted butter
1½ ounces (40g) flour
1½ cups (375ml) fish stock (or more)
   a few sprigs parsley and celery leaves
1 clove garlic, bruised
1 small onion, finely chopped
   a few white peppercorns, bruised
2 bay leaves
¼–½ cup (60–125ml) heavy cream
   salt and freshly ground pepper,
   preferably white

Melt the butter in a heavy-based pot and add the flour, stirring constantly. Stir over moderately low heat for a few minutes, so the flour will lose its raw taste. Remove the pot from the heat and pour in the fish stock all at once, stirring vigorously. Return to moderate heat and stir until the mixture starts to boil and thicken.

Add the parsley and celery leaves, garlic, onion, peppercorns, and bay leaves and simmer very gently for 20 minutes, stirring frequently. If the sauce becomes too thick, add a little more fish stock.

Strain the sauce to remove all the solids and return to a clean pan. Add half the heavy cream, or more if the sauce is too thick. Cook gently for 5 minutes, and add salt and pepper.

Surrender to Summer

As the summer heats up, the dappled shade of a breezy garden beckons. A salad buffet lets everyone enjoy the weather and the garden display at its peak.

POMMES DE TERRE TSARINE

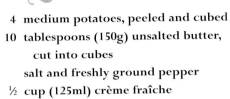

4 medium potatoes, peeled and cubed
10 tablespoons (150g) unsalted butter, cut into cubes
    salt and freshly ground pepper
½ cup (125ml) crème fraîche
6½ ounces (200g) caviar

Boil the potatoes in lightly salted boiling water until tender. Drain and return to the pan and place over low heat for 1 minute to dry completely.

Mash until smooth. (Don't use a food processor, this makes potatoes pasty.) Beat in the butter pieces, one by one, with a wooden spoon. Season with salt and pepper.

Spoon servings of potato onto heated plates and make a hollow in the middle. Fill with a dollop of crème fraîche and top this with a spoonful of caviar.

Serves 4

SALAD BUFFET

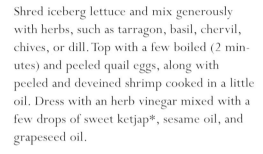

The following salads are a refreshing way to celebrate the bounty of summer. Add as much or as little of each ingredient as you like, and feel free to substitute at will.

Pasta and Mozzarella Salad

Choose your favorite short pasta and cook in plenty of salted boiling water until *al dente*. Drain and cool. Mix with briefly cooked and refreshed green beans, snow peas, peas, halved cherry tomatoes, fresh basil, and pieces of mozzarella. Dress with a mixture of extra virgin olive oil, vinegar, salt, and freshly ground black pepper.

Salad with Grilled Asparagus

Rinse and spin-dry several types of lettuce. Cook cubes of bacon until crisp. Steam white or green asparagus until just tender but still crisp, and then quickly grill it on a stovetop grill, to get a smoky flavor. Combine these ingredients with toasted pine nuts and finely sliced celery. Dress with walnut or hazelnut oil and a fruity vinegar.

Potato Salad with Smoked Salmon

Mix equal quantities of mayonnaise and crème fraîche, some salt and pepper, and a little snipped chives or dill. Serve on top of crisp pieces of bacon, a good quantity of cooked potato slices, and lastly, small slices of smoked salmon. You can make the same dish with shrimp, smoked halibut, or trout.

Herb and Shrimp Salad

Shred iceberg lettuce and mix generously with herbs, such as tarragon, basil, chervil, chives, or dill. Top with a few boiled (2 minutes) and peeled quail eggs, along with peeled and deveined shrimp cooked in a little oil. Dress with an herb vinegar mixed with a few drops of sweet ketjap*, sesame oil, and grapeseed oil.

* Ketjap is an Indonesian sweet soy sauce, available in Asian food stores. If it is not available, use soy sauce mixed with a little brown sugar.

Cucumber, Tomato, and Crab Salad

Make dressing first by mixing raspberry vinegar, a few drops of balsamic vinegar, walnut or hazelnut oil, and salt and pepper to taste. Set aside.

Make 2 inch × ¼ inch (5cm × ½cm) cucumber strips, unpeeled; peel a few tomatoes, seed, and cut into strips; cook a handful of fresh peas. Sauté 2 finely chopped shallots gently in a tiny amount of butter until soft.

Cut cooked crab into bite-size pieces, season with salt and pepper, add to the pan with the shallots, and warm through. Add the peas, and remove from heat. Add the tomato and cucumber. Spoon into a shallow bowl, warm the dressing, and pour over. Serve immediately or at room temperature.

Eating Out

On long summer days, every meal can be eaten outside. Savory dishes such as Vegetable Quiche and Veal Rolls are just as delicious once they've cooled a bit as when served warm from the oven. So they travel well to a table set in the garden, or in picnic baskets to a blanket beneath a shade tree.

VEGETABLE QUICHE

1 package frozen puff pastry
2 leeks, white parts only, finely sliced
2 red peppers, seeds and membranes removed, 1 finely chopped, 1 cut into strips, for garnish
1 green pepper, seeds and membranes removed, finely chopped
5 ounces (150g) button mushrooms, halved if large, and a few extra, thinly sliced, for garnish
1 onion, chopped
1 cup (250g) cottage cheese
1 cup (250g) ricotta cheese
2 ounces (50g) grated cheddar cheese
5 eggs
¼ cup (60ml) heavy cream
parsley
salt and freshly ground black pepper

Preheat oven to 350°F (180°C).

Roll the pastry out to fit a 9-inch (23cm) lightly greased tart pan with removable bottom. Line with foil and pastry weights or dried beans and bake for 10 minutes. Remove foil and pastry weights and return to the oven for 5 to 10 minutes or until the pastry starts to color.

Spread the leeks and the chopped red and green peppers into the pastry shell and tuck the mushrooms in between.

Combine the onion, cottage cheese, ricotta cheese, cheddar cheese, eggs, heavy cream, and parsley in a food processor and process until smooth. Season with salt and pepper. Pour over the vegetables in the pastry shell.

Cover with foil and bake for 45 minutes or until the filling has set. Remove foil for the last 20 minutes. Serve warm, or at room temperature.

Serves 6 to 8

VEAL ROLLS

1 pound (500g) chopped veal
1 egg, lightly beaten
1 tablespoon Dijon mustard, plus extra for rolls
2 tablespoons mixed chopped fresh tarragon and thyme
1 small onion, finely chopped
1 tablespoon sweet ketjap*
2 tablespoons sherry
2 tablespoons heavy cream
    salt and freshly ground black pepper
2 tablespoons olive oil
8 small bread rolls

Preheat oven to 300°F (150°C).

Combine the veal in a large bowl with the egg, 1 tablespoon mustard, herbs, onion, ketjap, sherry, and heavy cream, and season with salt and pepper.

Heat the oil in a frying pan and add the veal mixture. Sauté until the veal is no longer pink and is cooked through.

Cut the bread rolls in half horizontally, leaving the bottoms intact, but removing most of the crumb from the top. Spread a little mustard on both sides and divide the meat among the bottom halves. Replace the tops and place in the oven for about 15 minutes to heat through. Serve immediately.

Serves 8

Ketjap is an Indonesian sweet soy sauce, available in Asian food stores. If not available, use soy sauce with a little brown sugar.

Blue
Surge

Great wands of brilliant blue make the Chinese forget-me-not stand out at the back of a border, where it will stridently overrule other plants if its exuberance is not curbed. Still, it's hard to deny such robust charm.

Earthly
Gifts

The bounty of the garden can make a display for your own pleasure or a glorious gift— for new neighbors, dear friends, elderly relatives—anyone you care for. A harvest basket brimming with good health and the cheer of bright blossoms is the ideal way to express your wishes for prosperity and joy.

Popping Up Again

Summer is graced with poppies, here California poppies, which belong to the genus Eschscholzia. Hot, dry, sandy conditions suit this short-lived perennial (it is planted as an annual in colder climates). The sepal cap that encloses the California poppy's petals is "popped" as the colors unfurl.

Rosy Apricots

In nature the color apricot has the most subtle beauty—it is not a monotone, but rather a gradual scale from pale cream to dusky red.

Roses and pomegranates show this extraordinary array of color at a time when gooseberries also show a red-tinged cheek.

A cake, bought from your favorite pastry shop, can be adorned with rose

petals. Flowers and petals may be frosted with a thin layer of icing—

for this purpose the roses should be fragrant, or they won't have a pleasant

flavor. Apricot-colored roses—including 'Gloire de Dijon' and 'Alchymist'

—are very fragrant, so they provide ideal flowers for frosting and nibbling.

The Apple and Mint Garden

The very words "apple" and "mint," here inscribed above the garden gate, are evocative of freshness and greenery. Late summer also yields elderberries, which add wonderful flavor to drinks, jellies, and syrups. The marble table with wrought-iron base has a permanent place in the garden—it serves as an elegant perch for trays of cordials poured from old glass decanters.

APPLE AND MINT JELLY

- 2 pounds (1kg) Granny Smith apples
- 1½ cups (375ml) apple cider vinegar
- ¼ cup mint leaves
- 1½ pounds (750g) sugar
- 2 tablespoons freshly squeezed lemon juice
- 6 tablespoons mint flowers

Cut apples into pieces and combine in a pan with the vinegar and an equal amount of water and half the mint leaves. Bring to a boil and simmer very gently for 30 minutes. Strain into a bowl, through a cheesecloth-lined colander, for 2 hours.

Measure the liquid and add ½ cup (125g) sugar for every ½ cup (125ml) liquid. Add the lemon juice and bring to a boil. Boil vigorously for 4 minutes.

Allow to cool a little, then add the mint flowers and remaining leaves, and pour into three 1-cup (250ml) sterilized jars.

Makes three 1-cup (250ml) jars

White on White

In the white garden the warmer weather has worked its magic with a new riot of pale flowering. Above the throng, Japanese angelica (Aralia elata) fans out fernlike leaves to cradle creamy white flower tufts. Wild hydrangea (Hydrangea arborescens), with its green-tinged blossoms, occupies the garden's middle ground. The white torches of moth mullein (Verbascum blattaria) and the pure white bells of Campanula latifolia 'Alba' seem to glow in the summer sun, while the low-growing baby's breath (Gypsophila) turns its miniature petals to the sky.

A Posy of Pastels

Like giant green powder puffs, three acacia bushes trained into standards give form to the outer edges of a pastel palette. Phlox, astilbe, and tall, feathery meadowsweet (Filipendula) provide the pinks. For silver we look to artemisia. Deep purple monkshood (Aconitum) provides a darker counterpoint, while lady's mantle (Alchemilla) spreads its soft yellow-green flowers across the foreground.

You can pick wonderful bouquets from a garden like this without robbing it bare. The beautiful floral arrangement forms a backdrop for a still life of fruit, with quinces adding their fragrance to the flowers.

Potato Passions

Freshly dug potatoes—pearly, pink, smooth brown, or grubby with earth—are one of the delights of the garden. Plant a variety to suit your purpose: the waxy types for dishes requiring thin-sliced or grated potatoes; firm whites for salad; starchy, flavorful varieties for soup and purée. . . .

POTATO AND CELERIAC QUICHE

1½ pounds (750g) celeriac, peeled and cut
     into large pieces
2 cups (500 ml) heavy cream
     salt and freshly ground black pepper
1¼ pound (625g) large potatoes,
     coarsely grated
¼ pound (125g) sliced bacon, chopped
1 onion, very thinly sliced
5 egg yolks, plus 2 whole eggs
     9-inch (23cm) pre-baked puff
     pastry shell

Combine the celeriac and 1 cup (250ml) of
the heavy cream in a pan and simmer until
the celeriac is tender, about 20–30 minutes,
stirring occasionally. Purée celeriac with a
little cream and season to taste with salt and
pepper. Measure 1 cup (250ml) of this purée
and combine in a bowl with the raw potato.
Reserve the remaining purée for another use.
Preheat oven to 350°F (180°C).

Cook the bacon in a frying pan until crisp.
Remove with a slotted spoon and drain on
paper towels. Add to the potato mixture with
the onion.

Beat together the yolks, whole eggs, and
the remaining 1 cup (250ml) heavy cream
until smooth, season with salt and pepper.
Fold into the vegetable mixture and spoon
into the puff pastry shell. Cover with foil and
bake for 30–45 minutes, or until set and the
potato is cooked. Remove the foil and bake for
another 10 minutes or until golden on top.

Serves 6 to 8

POTATO SALAD

1 pound (500g) small new potatoes,
     cleaned but unpeeled
2 tablespoons (30g) unsalted butter
4 shallots, peeled and finely chopped
¼ pound (125g) mushrooms, cleaned
     and coarsely chopped
     salt and freshly ground black pepper
¼ cup black olives, pitted and halved
3 tablespoons chopped chives
⅓ cup (75ml) mayonnaise

Boil or steam the potatoes until tender, then
drain. Shake briefly in the pan over the heat
to dry out completely. They can be used in
the salad as they are, or quickly fried in some
oil until golden. In either case, set aside until
needed.

Melt the butter in a frying pan, add the
shallots, and cook until soft, about 5 minutes.
Add the mushrooms and cook just until they
start to release their juice. Season with salt
and pepper.

Add the olives and chives to the lukewarm
potatoes, and mix well with the mayonnaise.
Sprinkle the mushroom mixture on top.

Serves 4

POMMES DE TERRE TSARINE SNACK

Make the Pommes de Terre Tsarine recipe on page 58 and serve as tiny individual servings on a spoon: spoon a small amount of potato purée onto a spoon, top with a little crème fraîche and caviar or salmon eggs.

VICHYSSOISE

3   tablespoons (45g) unsalted butter
1   large onion, chopped
2   pounds (1kg) white of leeks, sliced
2   pounds (1kg) potatoes, peeled and
      coarsely chopped
4   cups (1 litre) chicken stock
1   cup (250ml) crème fraîche
1   cup (250ml) heavy cream
    salt and freshly ground pepper
    freshly squeezed lemon juice

Melt the 3 tablespoons (45g) butter in a large pot. Add the onion and leek, and cook over low heat until soft, about 5 minutes. Add the potatoes and stock, bring to a boil, and simmer until potatoes are tender.

Cool until just warm, then purée. Stir in the crème fraîche and cool completely. Stir in the heavy cream and season with salt, pepper, and lemon juice. Serve the soup cold in summer, or warm in cool weather.

A nice addition to the cold soup is some finely cubed cucumber, and for special occasions, a spoonful of caviar or salmon eggs.

Serves 6 to 8

POTATO CHIPS WITH FRESH SALMON

2   potatoes, very thinly sliced, preferably
      in a food processor
    sunflower or peanut oil
4   salmon fillets, 4 ounces (100g) each
    salt and freshly ground black pepper
2   tablespoons (30g) unsalted butter
    Beurre Blanc (recipe follows)

Arrange about 5 to 6 still-moist potato slices, (so they'll stick together) overlapping, to make a flower shape. Heat about ½ inch (1cm) oil in a small frying pan and slide in 1 flower shape at a time. Cook until golden brown and cooked through. The overlapping pieces will take longer to cook. Remove with a spatula and drain on paper towels.

Cut the salmon fillets in half horizontally and season with salt and pepper. Heat the butter in a heavy-based frying pan and cook the salmon fillets over moderately high heat on one side only, until brown. The other side will be just warmed through and nearly cooked, which is exactly how salmon should be.

On each plate, layer the ingredients in this order: first potato, then salmon, potato, salmon, and potato. Serve with Beurre Blanc.

Serves 4

Beurre Blanc

Beurre blanc is an emulsion—a mixture of two liquids that normally will not combine smoothly. You can emulsify by slowly (drop by drop in the beginning) adding one ingredient to the other, stirring vigorously. Minute droplets of one liquid are dispersed and suspended throughout the other. The final mixture should be thick and satiny. Two other examples of emulsion sauces are mayonnaise (uncooked) and hollandaise (cooked).

  3 **shallots, finely chopped**
  3 **tablespoons white wine vinegar**
  ½ **cup (125ml) white wine or water**
10 **tablespoons (250g) unsalted butter,**
     cut into small cubes, at room
     temperature
     salt and freshly ground white pepper
     freshly squeezed lemon juice

Combine the shallots in a pan with the vinegar and wine or water. Bring to a boil and reduce by half. Strain and discard the shallots. Turn heat to a simmer and start adding the butter piece by piece. Whisk vigorously until all the butter has been added. Season with salt, pepper, and lemon juice.

Serves 4 to 6

A Sprinkle of Summer Rain

When rain wraps the garden

in mist, the air fills with released

fragrances. Leaves and eaves

rattle under raindrops. Move a

table close to the open doors

and soak up the heady scent

of the refreshed garden.

In the Pink

Cottage pinks (Dianthus plumarius) grow in clumps like delicately embroidered cushions. This beautifully scented flower is a prolific self-seeder. It also has culinary uses: the petals add a pleasant clovelike flavor to fruit salads and savory dishes. You will find that cottage pinks are often grown as perennials in warmer climates.

Roses, too, confirm the old belief that "if it smells good, it must taste good." The roses pictured here were bred by David Austin in the 1960s to honor the culinary luminary Constance Spry. Although 'Constance Spry' flowers just once in a season, its abundant display and delicious fragrance have won devotees around the world.

Lacemakers

The airy white flowers of bishop's weed (Ammi majus) dance in the breeze. Naturalized throughout much of North America, this tall but delicate-looking perennial grows in great hazy swaths under the prolific lilac-colored rose 'Veilchenblau'. Better known as a climber, 'Veilchenblau' is here trained as a standard, arching its blooms over the garden.

A pretty bouquet repeats the colors of this garden corner, with ornamental onion, sweet pea, and acanthus in an artichoke pitcher.

A Savory Tea

Gazing balls, also called witches' balls, were set about in olden times to send the cackling creatures fleeing at the sight of their own reflections. This one reflects only a blue dome of sky and the beauty of a lush garden.

Crisp toasts with salmon, rounds topped with scrambled egg and caviar, mini-quiches, mussels on the shell…an assortment of savory morsels is quickly assembled with the simple recipes on the following pages.

Fresh Offerings

The tea party continues, with mini-pizzas, bacon sandwiches, and toast spread with creamy avocado and dollops of salmon roe. The garden inspires our choice of table decoration—including the leaf-shaped platters and garnishes of fresh herbs such as purple basil. The Earl of Sandwich would be well satisfied with the evolution of these delicacies.

SANDWICHES

Toast a large quantity of crustless white bread. Make a variety of the following sandwiches:

- Smoked salmon sandwich. Place lettuce leaves on the bread, drape a slice of salmon over this, and top with a paper-thin slice of lemon. Season with freshly ground black pepper.
- Bacon sandwich. Fry bacon slices in a well-seasoned frying pan over moderate heat, without fat, until crisp and golden brown. Drain on paper towels before using. Brush toast with a thin layer of mustard and top with lettuce and bacon; finish off with another slice of toast.
- Avocado sandwich. Press the avocado flesh through a sieve or mash it very well. Add a little heavy cream and season with lemon juice, Tabasco, salt, and freshly ground black pepper. Pile onto toast rounds and garnish with salmon eggs and basil.
- Scrambled egg and caviar sandwich. Lightly beat a few eggs with a little heavy cream, salt, and lots of freshly ground black pepper. Cook this in unsalted butter over very low heat, scraping the bottom of the pan when the mixture sets. As soon as the egg loses its liquidity, spoon onto toast. Top with a small dollop of caviar.

MINI-PIZZAS

Buy a ball of fresh pizza dough from your local pizzeria or prepare some yourself from a package. Make small balls and press these into 3-inch (8cm) circles. Brush with a little tomato purée and some pesto, then top with thin onion rings, small pieces of tomato, a slice of mozzarella, olives, and basil. Grind black pepper over the top and bake in a 350°F (180°C) oven for 10 minutes or until the dough is cooked. Serve warm or cold.

Savoring Twilight

As day turns into night, the garden becomes an enchanted setting for an elegant dinner with friends.

MUSSELS IN HERB BUTTER

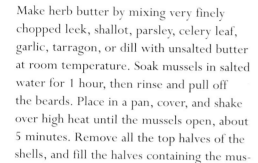

Make herb butter by mixing very finely chopped leek, shallot, parsley, celery leaf, garlic, tarragon, or dill with unsalted butter at room temperature. Soak mussels in salted water for 1 hour, then rinse and pull off the beards. Place in a pan, cover, and shake over high heat until the mussels open, about 5 minutes. Remove all the top halves of the shells, and fill the halves containing the mussels with herb butter. Sprinkle with dry bread crumbs, place on a tray under a hot broiler. Remove when the butter bubbles and the top is golden.

RAVIOLI

Finely chop and combine 1 onion, prosciutto, shiitake mushrooms (or substitute your favorite mushrooms), torn basil leaves, and salt and freshly ground pepper in a frying pan with oil. Cook over medium heat, stirring constantly, for 2 minutes. Allow to cool.

Meanwhile, lightly beat 1 egg white and use to brush around the edges of 1 wonton wrapper (available at Asian food stores). Place a teaspoonful of the filling in the middle, then brush the edges of another wrapper, lay the second wrapper over the first, press to expel any air, and securely seal the edges. Use a round cutter to make round ravioli. Continue with the remaining filling and wrappers. Bring some water to a near-boil and cook the ravioli in batches for 5 minutes. Remove with a slotted spoon and serve immediately.

MINI-QUICHE WITH SALMON

Make quiche pastry in small tart tins and fill with the cream and egg mixture, seasoned with salt and pepper (see pages 61 and 79 for quiche and pastry recipes and method). Drop small pieces of smoked salmon into this mixture and bake in a 350°F (180°C) oven for 10–15 minutes or until the custard has set.

Contrasting Views

Garden furniture not only provides a welcome place to sit, but can divide the garden into areas for entertaining. Similarly, architectural decorations provide focal points that draw the eye into their sphere. Here, the contrast of stone and foliage sets up an interesting counterpoint. A pale green broccoli soup, made robust with bacon, beckons us to lunch.

CREAMED BROCCOLI SOUP

- 4 cups (1 litre) chicken stock
- 1 cup (250ml) heavy cream
- 2 large broccoli heads, divided into small florets, stalks discarded
- ½ cup (125ml) crème fraîche
  salt and freshly ground black pepper
- ¼ pound (125g) thinly sliced lean bacon
- 1 large onion, thinly sliced

Combine the stock and the heavy cream in a saucepan and bring to a boil. Add two-thirds of the broccoli florets. Cook for 5 minutes, then remove the florets with a slotted spoon and purée with a little of the liquid. Return to the saucepan. Add the crème fraîche, simmer gently for 10 minutes, and season with the salt and pepper.

Meanwhile, cook the bacon in a frying pan until golden brown and crisp. Drain on paper towels and keep warm. Add the onion to the frying pan and cook in the bacon fat over high heat until golden brown. Remove and keep warm. Add the reserved broccoli florets to the pan and sauté quickly, until crisp-tender.

Serve the soup garnished with the onion, bacon, and crisp broccoli florets.

Serves 6

Water Gardens

The romantic possibilities of bridges can be explored in gardens with watercourses. Even a small pond brims with opportunities to admire the swoop of dragonflies, the crowning glory of water lilies, and the unfurling of arums. Enjoy an idyllic waterside lunch of lobster and a good bottle of chilled wine.

LOBSTER WITH LEEK, CURRY, AND VANILLA

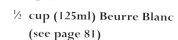

½ cup (125ml) Beurre Blanc
  (see page 81)
2 inches (5cm) of vanilla bean
1 cooked lobster, halved
1 leek, white part julienned into
    2-inch (5cm) pieces
2 tablespoons olive oil
1 teaspoon best quality curry powder
½ cup (125ml) heavy cream
    salt and freshly ground black pepper

Warm the Beurre Blanc over simmering water and add the vanilla bean. Take the lobster meat from the shells, keeping the shells intact, and remove the meat from the claws.

Combine the leek in a pan with the oil and cook, stirring frequently, for 5 minutes or until soft. Stir in the curry powder. Add the lobster meat and toss over the heat until warm and colored by the curry. Pour in the heavy cream and cook until reduced. Remove the pan from the heat.

Remove the lobster meat from the pan and return to the shells. Add the Beurre Blanc to the still-warm pan. Stir vigorously, then remove the vanilla bean. Spoon the sauce over the lobster.

Serves 2

A Rose Is a Rose…

No flower is more evocative, none appears more often in prose and poetry throughout the ages than the rose.

Here, a tumble of roses is held aloft by the weathered arm of a stone cherub.

Over the Top

Climbing and rambling roses riot over arches, gateways, and pergolas. Teamed with clematis, the roses make a garland with which to crown summer. Two or three rose varieties climbing over and through a lattice of wire create a living tapestry of color.

Roses are at their most fragrant just when they start to wilt. It is said that the Russian czars used to put a waterless vessel of perfect blossoms beside each place setting at the table, so that guests could enjoy the aroma of wilting flowers along with their food and wine. It is best to frost a rose that is just on the verge of wilting.

TO FROST ROSES

Frost petals or whole flowers of fragrant roses, because these will have the best flavor. And always make sure that the flowers have not been sprayed with insecticide.

Lightly beat egg whites with a fork and paint the petals or whole flowers very thinly but meticulously, on all sides with the egg white. Sprinkle all over with fine sugar and shake off the excess. Then place in a 100°F (50°C) oven with the door ajar, until the roses are dried and the whole house smells heavenly.

A Full-Blown Farewell

When the blossom's fragrance is at its height and before it loses its profusion of petals to the wind,

the rose in full bloom takes glorious pride of place in the garden.

Purple Poetry

There are many shades of purple, from palest mauve to deepest grape, with which to color the garden. Lilac is an obvious and appealing choice. Geraniums, phlox, pansies, bellflowers, and lobelias come in royal tones. Salvia moves toward blue, astilbe is hot-pink verging on deep red, and the dark-stemmed marjoram called 'Hopley's' is much loved by bees and butterflies. Sow a sprinkling of purple toadflax and Allium sphaerocephalon between it all to complete the purple poetry.

For the Bees

The tall spires of hollyhock lure bees, which like to bumble and scramble deep into each bloom for a good dusting of pollen. And after a few seasons of self-seeding, the unruly centranthus will take possession of the cracks and crevices of a stone wall, attracting not only bees but butterflies to its craning heads of pink blossom.

Baskets of Blooms

To completely envelop an area with flowers, display some in pots set on walls or pedestals to raise them above the ground. Hang baskets cascading with flowers from pergolas or tree branches. Pansies, heliotrope, and petunias flourish in these pots and urns, while shade-loving impatiens drops in under the cover of climbing roses and clematis.

Rosehips and Bells

'Alba' rugosa rose begins the color show of autumn with fat orange-red hips, intriguing in display with the green bells of Humulus. *Rosehips make delicious, tangy jams and jellies to spread on toast, or to accompany poultry and game.*

In another combination of green and orange, guinea fowl is simply roasted and served on a bed of vegetables with tarragon sauce.

GUINEA FOWL WITH TARRAGON CREAM SAUCE AND VEGETABLES

1¼ pounds (625g) mixed green beans and snow peas
   small bunch baby carrots
2 guinea fowl, halved
   salt and freshly ground black pepper
5 tablespoons (75g) unsalted butter
   small bunch scallions, cut diagonally
   13-ounce (400g) can baby corn cobs, drained

Tarragon Cream Sauce

2 cups (500ml) chicken stock
1 small onion, finely chopped
1 bay leaf
1 carrot, chopped
   white part of half a leek, chopped
1 ounce (30g) bacon, chopped
   small handful of parsley and celery leaves
   a few sprigs of tarragon
½ cup (125ml) heavy cream
2 tablespoons (30g) unsalted butter, in pieces

Plunge the green vegetables and the carrots into a large pan of lightly salted boiling water, return to a boil, and cook for 4 minutes. Drain and refresh under cold running water.

Season the guinea fowl with salt and pepper, melt 3 tablespoons (45g) butter in a frying pan, and add the fowl. Brown the skin side well, then turn the heat down and simmer until cooked through, about 15 minutes.

Meanwhile, make the sauce by combining the stock, onion, bay leaf, carrot, leek, bacon, and herbs in a pan and simmer gently for 30 minutes without a lid. Add the heavy cream and simmer 15 minutes more. Taste, and if the tarragon flavor is not strong enough, add a little more. Strain the sauce and season. Stir in the butter, piece by piece, and keep warm.

Melt the remaining 2 tablespoons (30g) butter in a frying pan, add the precooked vegetables, and stir over moderate heat until warmed through. Add the scallions and well-drained baby corn cobs and heat through. Arrange the vegetables on a heated platter, top with the carved fowl, and spoon on the sauce.

Serves 4

Late-Summer Scents

Peaches and apricots are at their luscious best in late summer. Ivy is ever ready to decorate the table, looking fresh and festive against a white cloth. Carafes hold the pick of the garden—purple and white Lisianthus in one, and blue and white cornflowers in the other.

At a crossroad on the garden path a stone pedestal holds a profusion of the misty blues and soft pinks of the season.

A Slow-Cooked Oven Stew

Three different meats go into the pot, together with baby turnips, carrots, pickled onions, herbs, and beer, to cook for a leisurely few hours. Return from an afternoon's pruning to lift the lid on a savory dish, mellow in taste and cooked to tenderness—the hallmarks of a good stew.

POT-AU-FEU WITH BEER

The flavor of most stews improves after a day, and this one is no exception.

1 **pound (500g) each of beef, veal, and pork stewing meat, cut into 3-inch (8cm) pieces**
  salt and freshly ground black pepper
2 **tablespoons (30g) unsalted butter**
2 **tablespoons olive oil**
2 **bay leaves**
2 **large onions, sliced**
2 **large cloves garlic, finely chopped**
¼ **pound (150g) turnips, coarsely chopped**
¼ **pound (150g) carrots, thickly sliced**
5 **ounces (150g) pickled onions, well rinsed**
2 **bottles of beer, 12 ounces (375ml) each**

Preheat oven to 325°F (160°C).

Season the meat with salt and pepper. Combine the butter and oil in a large frying pan and when the foam starts to subside, add the meat and cook over high heat until golden brown on all sides. You shouldn't crowd the pan, so this may have to be done in batches.

Arrange the meat in an ovenproof dish and tuck in the bay leaves. Without cleaning the frying pan first, add the sliced onion to it and cook until soft and golden, about 5 minutes. Add the garlic and cook for 1 more minute. Add the turnips, carrots, and pickled onions, stir briefly over moderate heat, then add to the meat.

Add the beer to the same frying pan and heat, scraping up any browned bits. Pour enough over the meat and vegetables to nearly cover them. Cover the dish securely and bake for about 2½ hours or until all the ingredients are very tender.

Halfway through the cooking time you may add pieces of potato or soaked, dried beans. Also add any herbs on hand. Allow the dish to stand for 10 minutes before serving.

Serves 6 to 8

Tip: If you have time, cool the whole dish to room temperature, then leave in the refrigerator overnight. The next day you can remove any fat that has congealed on top.

Golden Harvest

The colors of the sun shine from a bouquet of zinnias, Lisianthus alstroemeria, *ranunculus, the yellow umbels of achillea, and plumes of goldenrod. Gooseberries and the disks of the money plant add green, and ripe, sun-drenched strawberries contribute a luscious red.*

Elsewhere, loosestrife fills a field with glowing torches.

The Garden Gate

A romantic garden needs a romantic gateway, like this one festooned with roses and flanked by pots filled with ornamental red cabbages and rich purple petunias. A carpet of bellflowers spreads away to either side. And because there is only filtered light, spurred snapdragons have pulled themselves up to their full height with the support of the gate, adding their pastel spikes to the garden scene.

Sunflowers

Oh, those sunny faces! The glorious nodding heads of giant sunflowers brighten the garden until autumn when birds make a feast of the seeds. Tall varieties tower over visitors while dwarf types grow happily in pots or in the mixed border. Few other flowers inspire as much joy as these brash garden denizens.

Pumpkins and Squash

As summer comes to an end, we appreciate the bountiful harvest of pumpkins and squash. Mellow in tone and flavor, their variety of shape and color makes them ideal subjects for display.

PUMPKIN SOUP

Serve this soup with plenty of crusty bread and butter.

- 2 pounds (1kg) pumpkin, peeled and diced
- 1 pound (500g) potatoes, peeled and diced
- 2 large onions, thickly sliced
- 6 cups (1.5 litres) chicken stock or water
  salt and freshly ground black pepper
  sour cream, dry sherry, or white wine (optional)

Combine the pumpkin, potatoes, onions, and stock or water in a large pan with salt to taste. Bring to a boil and simmer until all the vegetables are tender, about 20–30 minutes. Purée and season with salt and pepper. Serve with a dollop of sour cream or a dash of sherry or white wine, if desired.

Serves 6 to 8

Late-Season Picnic

Take every opportunity to be outside, because soon enough the changing season will force you back to the warmth of the kitchen and fireside. Dinners, lunches, brunches—make them portable, to be enjoyed in the open air while the weather is still favorable.

CHICKEN WITH GARLIC AND OLIVES

Spread the soft garlic on thick slices of crusty bread.

1   cup (250ml) extra virgin olive oil
16   drumsticks
    salt and freshly ground black pepper
1   head garlic (or more), divided into cloves and peeled
6   ounces (180g) black olives, preferably kalamata, pitted
1   cup (250ml) red wine

Preheat oven to 450°F (230°C).

Heat 3 tablespoons of the oil in a large frying pan and when hot but not smoking, add the chicken and quickly cook on all sides until golden. (If the pan is not large enough, this may be done in batches.) Remove chicken from the frying pan and place in a baking dish, seasoned with salt and pepper and scattered with the garlic and olives.

Mix the remaining oil with the red wine and pour over the chicken. Wrap the whole dish securely in foil and bake for 1 hour. Remove the foil and bake another 10 minutes, or until the chicken is golden and crisp.

Serves 8

Autumn's Abundance

When autumn brings too many apples, we use some to make pretty garlands, accented with the lovely yellow-green flowers of lady's mantle. Honeysuckle adds fragrance to a horn of plenty, the symbol of abundance.

The Apple Bowl

An overflowing basket of apples is a sure sign that autumn has arrived.

Display the rosy-cheeked beauties with glossy ivy or bake them into simple

but spectacular desserts. Tarte Tatin, the famous French upside-down apple

tart, was created by the Tatin sisters, spinsters who made a living by selling

their tarts around the Loire Valley.

TARTE TATIN

10 tablespoons (150g) unsalted butter,
   cut into slices

1¼ cup (300g) sugar

4 pounds (2kg) firm apples, such as
   Granny Smith or Golden Delicious,
   peeled, cored, quartered, and cut
   into ½-inch (1cm)-thick slices

1 package frozen puff pastry
   ice cream or crème fraîche, to serve

Preheat oven to 400°F (200°C).

Cover the bottom of an 11-inch (28cm) one-piece tart pan with the butter, and sprinkle with the sugar. Cover with the apple slices, overlapping them and making sure there are no gaps. Bake for 20 minutes. Remove from the oven and allow the apples to cool. Increase the oven temperature to 425°F (220°C).

Roll out the puff pastry into a 12-inch (30cm) circle and drape over the cooled apples, tucking in the sides. Bake until the pastry starts to brown, then reduce oven temperature to 350°F (180°C) and bake another 15 minutes.

Remove and allow to cool slightly. Place a platter over the top of the pan and invert the tart. Serve warm, with a scoop of vanilla ice cream or a dollop of crème fraîche.

Serves 8

DUCK WITH APPLES, PEPPER, AND OLIVE SAUCE

2 duck breasts, bones removed
salt and freshly ground black pepper
3 tablespoons olive oil
1 small red pepper, seeds and membranes removed, chopped
1 ounce (30g) pitted and chopped kalamata olives
¼ cup (60ml) dry white wine
3 tablespoons (45g) unsalted butter
2 apples, cored and cut into thin wedges

Season the duck with salt and pepper, rubbing it in well. Heat the oil in a frying pan until hot but not smoking. Add the duck, skin side down, and cook over moderately high heat until browned. Reduce to a simmer, turn the duck over, and add the pepper, olives, and wine. Cover with a lid and cook gently until duck is tender, about 20–30 minutes.

Remove duck breasts from the pan and place briefly under a hot broiler, skin side up, to brown and crisp. Keep warm. Stir the contents of the pan over moderately high heat until the sauce slightly thickens.

Meanwhile, melt the butter in a frying pan, add the apples, and sauté over medium heat until the apples are tender, golden, and starting to crisp at the edges.

Slice the duck and serve on heated plates, pour over the pepper and olive sauce, and serve the apples on the side.

Serves 4

TOMATOES STUFFED WITH RATATOUILLE

This makes a simple side dish to serve with roast meat or grilled fish.

10 large tomatoes
3 tablespoons extra virgin olive oil
1 large onion, finely chopped
3 cloves garlic, finely chopped
1 green pepper diced
1 yellow pepper diced
1 red pepper diced
1 large zucchini, diced
1 medium eggplant, diced
3 tablespoons chopped flat parsley
salt and freshly ground black pepper

Remove a thin slice off the stem end of the tomatoes. Scoop the flesh and seeds out with a teaspoon without damaging the shell, discard the seeds, and place the flesh in a saucepan. Cook the flesh over low heat, breaking the tomato up with a wooden spoon, until tender, about 15 minutes. Push through a sieve and measure ½ cup of sauce.

Preheat oven to 400°F (200°C).

Combine the oil and onion in a frying pan and cook until onion is soft, stirring constantly, about 5 minutes. Add the garlic and stir another minute. Remove from pan with a slotted spoon and set aside in a bowl.

Now cook each vegetable in turn for 5 minutes or until crisp-tender. Remove from the pan and add to the bowl with onion when cooked. Stir in the tomato sauce and parsley, and season well with salt and pepper.

Place the tomato shells in a lightly greased baking dish and spoon the filling into the shells. Bake for 15 minutes or until heated through. Serve immediately.

Makes 10

Autumn

Leaves flutter from the trees and are swept into drifts by the breeze. Yellow-gold, bright orange, and burnished bronze add beauty to the autumn garden.

Once more the season's crop is earthy: nuts and mushrooms emerge in satisfying variety. A stillness settles on the garden, which has already begun the gathering of its resources to fuel the distant but inevitable burst of renewal.

Mushrooms

The resilient texture and almost meaty flavor of mushrooms have great appeal. The following recipes suggest using many different kinds of mushrooms. Buy whatever is freshest in the local markets, or go picking the fixings for one last picnic with a knowledgeable guide. A mixture of dried or fresh wild mushrooms—which are always quite expensive—with common button mushrooms is perfectly delicious. Substituting one mushroom for another will not have a detrimental effect on a dish, but will merely change the flavor.

TOURNEDOS WELLINGTON

One of the classic components of this dish is "duxelles," which is nothing more complicated than finely chopped mushrooms and shallots, briefly cooked in a little butter. Here we have added an unusual twist by including chopped almonds.

Duxelles

2 tablespoons (30g) unsalted butter
¼ pound (125g) field mushrooms, finely chopped
4 shallots, finely chopped
salt and freshly ground black pepper
1 ounce (30g) finely chopped almonds

Tournedos

4 beef tenderloin fillets, 7 ounces (200g) each
salt and freshly ground black pepper
2 tablespoons olive oil
2 tablespoons (30g) unsalted butter
4 slices goose liver, 2 ounces (60g), each
4 sheets puff pastry, 10 inches x 10 inches (25cm x 25cm), each
1 egg, separated
1 tablespoon water

Preheat oven to 400°F (200°C).

Make the duxelles first. Melt the butter in a small frying pan, then add the mushrooms and shallots, and cook over moderate heat, stirring frequently until soft, about 5 minutes. Season with salt and pepper and stir in the almonds.

To make the tournedos, rub the beef all over with salt and pepper. Combine the oil and butter in a small frying pan over moderately high heat, and when the butter foam starts to subside, add the beef and sear quickly on all sides. Drain on paper towels and, when slightly cool, place the goose liver on top, and then on each slice of liver place 2 tablespoons of the duxelles (freeze remaining duxelles for future use).

Place the pastry on top, fold underneath to enclose, and seal well at the bottom with the egg white, trimming corners if folds are too thick to make a neat ball. Beat the egg yolk lightly with 1 tablespoon water and brush over the top.

Place on a greased baking tray and bake for 20–30 minutes, or until the pastry is golden brown and the beef rare.

Note: If you like your beef more well done, cook a little longer before wrapping it in the pastry.

Serves 4

MUSHROOM TART

1 package frozen puff pastry
1 ounce (30g) dried porcini mushrooms
½ cup (125ml) chicken stock
½ cup (125ml) red wine
1 tablespoon (15g) unsalted butter
3 shallots or 1 small onion, finely chopped
5 ounces (150g) bacon, chopped
½ pound (250g) field mushrooms, roughly chopped
2 cups (500ml) heavy cream
4 eggs, plus 4 egg yolks
salt and freshly ground black pepper

Preheat oven to 375°F (190°C).

Defrost the pastry and roll out to line an 11-inch (28cm) tart pan with a removable bottom. Prick all over with a fork, then cover and refrigerate for 30 minutes. Line with foil and baking weights or dried beans and bake for 10 minutes, then remove foil and weights and bake until golden, about 10 minutes more. Set aside to cool. Turn oven off.

Place the porcini mushrooms in a bowl; bring the stock and wine to a near-boil and pour over the porcini. Let stand for 30 minutes, then strain and retain the liquid. Check the porcini for grit, chop coarsely, and set aside in a small bowl. Boil the liquid until reduced to a quarter, then strain carefully over the porcini in the bowl. Allow to cool.

Turn the oven on again to 400°F (200°C). Melt the butter in a large frying pan, add the

shallots, and cook over moderate heat until soft, about 5 minutes. Add the bacon and cook until the fat runs, then add the field mushrooms, and cook another 3–5 minutes or until the mushrooms are soft. Stir in the reserved porcini with their liquid and remove from the heat.

Combine the heavy cream, whole eggs, and egg yolks in a bowl and beat until smooth. Season with salt and pepper (keep in mind that the bacon is contributing a lot of salt). Stir in the cooled mushroom mixture and pour into the pre-baked tart shell in the tart pan.

Cover with foil and bake for 40 minutes or until the filling has set. Remove the foil and cook another 10 minutes or until golden brown. This tart is very good the next day, gently reheated in the oven.

Serves 6 to 8

CREAM OF MUSHROOM SOUP

- 3 tablespoons (45g) unsalted butter
- 1 large onion, chopped
- 2 cloves garlic, finely chopped
- 1 leek, white part only, sliced
- 1 ounce (30g) lean bacon, finely chopped
- 1½ ounces (45g) dried porcini mushrooms (soaked in warm water for 30 minutes then rinsed)
- 2 bay leaves
- 2 teaspoons mixed thyme and rosemary
  a few peppercorns
- 5 juniper berries, bruised
- ½ cup (125ml) red wine
- ½ cup (125ml) port
- 4 cups (1litre) beef stock
- 2 cups (500ml) heavy cream
  salt and freshly ground pepper
- 2 ounces (60g) fresh mushrooms

Melt 2 tablespoons (30g) of the butter in a large soup pan. Add the onion, garlic, leek, and bacon and cook over moderately low heat, stirring frequently, until the vegetables are soft, about 5–8 minutes.

Add the porcini, herbs, and spices and stir well for 1 minute. Add the wine and port, bring to a boil, and then add the beef stock.

Return to a boil, then simmer very gently for 1 hour. Add half of the heavy cream and simmer for 30 minutes.

Strain the soup and discard the contents of the sieve. If the color of the soup is too dark, add the other half of the heavy cream. Season with salt and pepper. Just before serving, melt the remaining 1 tablespoon (15g) butter in a frying pan and quickly fry the sliced fresh mushrooms, just until they start to release their juices. Place the mushroom slices on top of the soup to garnish.

Serves 4

CLEAR SOUP WITH MUSHROOMS AND GOOSE LIVER

- 1 ounce (30g) lean bacon, in 1 piece
- 4 cups (1litre) beef stock
- 1½ ounces (45g) dried porcini mushrooms
- 1 tablespoon (15g) unsalted butter
- 3 ounces (90g) fresh mushrooms, sliced
- 4 pieces goose liver, 1 oz (30g) each

Rub the inside of a frying pan with the bacon and set the pan aside. Place the bacon in a pot with the beef stock and porcini mushrooms, and simmer gently for 20 minutes.

Melt the butter in the bacon-rubbed frying pan, add the fresh mushrooms, and cook, stirring frequently, just until they start to release their liquid. Drain well on paper towels.

Strain the stock through muslin or cheesecloth, check the porcini for grit, and chop coarsely. Spoon the stock into bowls and add the porcini and fresh mushrooms. Place a slice of goose liver in the center and serve immediately.

Serves 4

BASIC STOCKS

Many soups use a basic stock of beef, veal, or chicken. With light-colored soups chicken or veal is generally used, while with darker-colored soups the stock is usually beef. Stocks are easy to make and exact quantities are unimportant. The number of bay leaves, juniper berries, peppercorns, or carrots is up to you.

To make 12 cups (3litres) of beef or veal stock, use 16 cups (4litres) water, 2 pounds (1kg) soup bones with meat, and 4 pounds (2kg) shanks with meat.

Chicken stock is even easier: use 2 pounds (1kg) chicken carcasses per 4 cups (1litre) water. Add vegetables such as onions, shallots, leeks, carrots, and celeriac and herbs such as parsley, celery leaves, sage, rosemary, thyme, bay leaves, and juniper berries, and, of course, salt and pepper. You may also cook a little piece of bacon along with it.

Bring the pot with carcasses and water to a boil and scoop off the foam. When no more foam develops, add the vegetables and herbs to taste. For example: use 3 leeks with greens, 5 onions, 5 shallots, 1 large carrot, 1½ pounds (250g) celeriac, all cut into large pieces; and 3 ounces (100g) bacon or smoked speck. Also add a mixed bunch of parsley and celery leaves, 6 sage leaves, 6 bay leaves, 10 juniper berries, and 10 peppercorns. (Don't put in salt now, this comes later.) Bring to a boil, then simmer for 4 hours, without a lid.

When ready, pour through a fine sieve into a bowl. Cool to room temperature, then refrigerate until a layer of congealed fat forms on top. Scoop this off and discard. Discard the carcasses and meat, as well.

Tip: For a dark stock, combine the meat and bones with onions in a greased baking dish, and bake in a 450°F (230°C) oven for 20 minutes or until browned. This will make a richly colored stock.

Index